W9-AYQ-949

The Life of
Abigail Adams

By Maria Nelson

Gareth Stevens
Publishing

Clifton Park - Halfmoon Public Library
475 Moe Road
Clifton Park, New York 12065

Please visit our website, www.garethstevens.com. For a free color catalog of all our high-quality books, call toll free 1-800-542-2595 or fax 1-877-542-2596.

Library of Congress Cataloging-in-Publication Data

Nelson, Maria.
  The life of Abigail Adams / Maria Nelson.
      p. cm. — (Famous lives)
  Includes index.
  ISBN 978-1-4339-6339-1 (pbk.)
  ISBN 978-1-4339-6340-7 (6-pack)
  ISBN 978-1-4339-6337-7 (library binding)
  1. Adams, Abigail, 1744-1818—Juvenile literature. 2. Presidents' spouses—United States—Biography—Juvenile literature. I. Title.
  E322.1.A38N45 2012
  973.4'4092—dc23
  [B]
                                        2011018182

First Edition 4|7|

Published in 2012 by
Gareth Stevens Publishing
111 East 14th Street, Suite 349
New York, NY 10003

Copyright © 2012 Gareth Stevens Publishing

Designer: Daniel Hosek
Editor: Kristen Rajczak

Photo credits: Cover, pp. 1, 5, 9, 13, 15, 21 Stock Montage/Getty Images; p. 7 De Agostini Picture Library/Getty Images; p. 11 Herbert Orth/Time & Life Pictures/Getty Images; p. 17 Hulton Archive/Getty Images; p. 19 Library of Congress, Prints and Photographs Division.

All rights reserved. No part of this book may be reproduced in any form without permission in writing from the publisher, except by a reviewer.

Printed in the United States of America

CPSIA compliance information: Batch #CW12GS: For further information contact Gareth Stevens, New York, New York at 1-800-542-2595.

Contents

Boldface words appear in the glossary.

Lady Adams

Abigail Adams was one of the most well-known women of her time. She wrote many letters that show people today what life was like when the United States was founded.

5

Early Life

Abigail was born in 1744. She grew up in Massachusetts. Abigail lived with her parents, brother, and three sisters. She was often sick and didn't go to school. Instead, Abigail learned at home. She read a lot!

18th-century Massachusetts

John Adams

Abigail married John Adams in 1764. John was a lawyer. John and Abigail wanted the **colonies** to be **independent**. In 1774, John went to Philadelphia to help write laws for the colonies. He **represented** Massachusetts.

John Adams

Abigail stayed at home. She raised their five children and ran their farm. Abigail and John wrote each other letters while he was gone. She wanted him to make women and men equal in the new country.

... he has distinguished himself in every engagement, by his coura[ge] and fortitude, by animating the soldiers & leading them on by his own example — a particular account of these dreadful, but I hope Glori[ous] Days will be transmitted you, no doubt in the exactest manner —

The race is not to the swift. nor the battle to the strong — but the God of Israel is he that giveth strength & power unto his people. Trust in him at all times ye people pour out your hearts before him, God is a refuge for us — Charlstown is laid in ashes — the Battle began upon our intrenchments upon Bunkers Hill, a Saturday morning about 3 oclock & has not ceased yet & tis now 3 oclock Sabbeth afternoon —

Tis expected they will come out over the Neck to night — & a dreadful Battle must ensue almighty God cover the heads of our Country men — & be a shield to our Dear Friends how many have fallen we know not — the constant roar of the cannon is so [distressing] that we cannot eat Drink or Sleep — may we be supported and sustaind in the dreadful conflict — I shall tarry here till tis thought unsafe by my Friends. & then I have secured myself a retreat at your Brothers who has kindly offerd me part of his House — I cannot compose myself to write any further at present — I will add more as I hear further —

Tuesday afternoon —

I have been so much agitated that I have not been able to write since Sabbeth Day — when I say that ten thousand reports are passing vague & [uncertain] ...

Overseas

When the **American Revolution** ended, John went to France and Britain to represent America. Abigail continued to write letters to him. She told him how the new government was doing.

13

Second Lady

Abigail became "second lady" in 1789. "Second lady" means wife of the vice president. John was George Washington's vice president for 8 years. Abigail traveled between their home in Massachusetts and the nation's capital during that time.

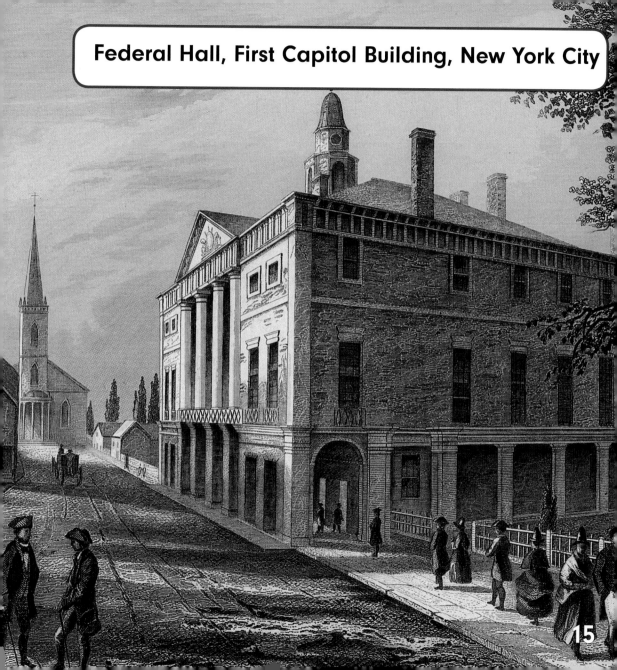

Federal Hall, First Capitol Building, New York City

15

First Lady

Abigail became First Lady of the United States when John became the nation's second president in 1797. The First Lady is the president's wife. John and Abigail were the first president and First Lady to live in the White House in Washington, DC!

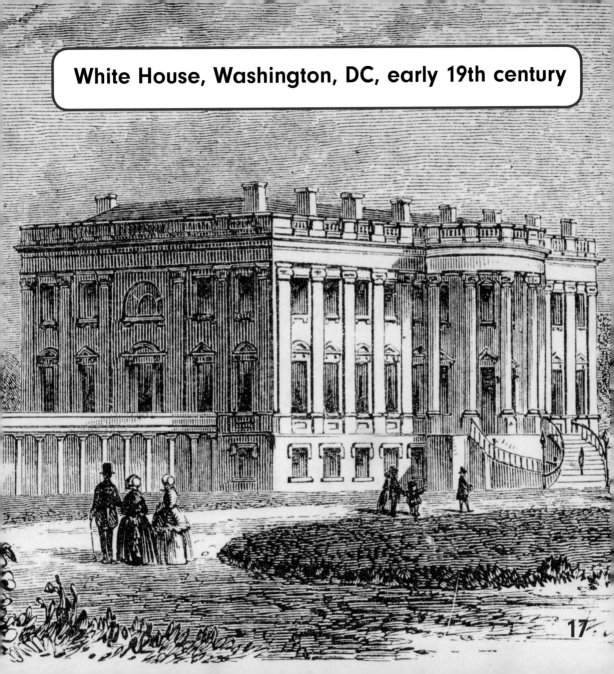

White House, Washington, DC, early 19th century

17

Abigail wasn't afraid to tell John what she thought of government actions. However, some people didn't think it was the First Lady's place to talk about **politics**. That didn't stop Abigail! She continued to speak her mind.

19

In Memory

Abigail and John moved back to Massachusetts after he lost the **election** of 1800. She wrote many letters to family and friends during the rest of her life. After Abigail died in 1818, her letters became an important part of history.

Timeline

—**1744**——Abigail is born.

—**1764**——Abigail marries John Adams.

—**1789**——Abigail becomes "second lady."

—**1797**——Abigail becomes First Lady.

—**1818**——Abigail dies.

Glossary

American Revolution: the war in which the colonists overthrew British control in order to choose a government run by the people

colony: a piece of land under the control of another country

election: the act of voting someone into a government position

independent: free

politics: the activities of the government and government officials

represent: to stand for or speak for. A person who represents is a representative.

For More Information

Books

Orr, Rachel. *Abigail Adams: Eyewitness to America's Birth*.
New York, NY: Collins, 2009.
Walsh, Francis. *Daring Women of the American Revolution*.
New York, NY: PowerKids Press, 2009.

Websites

The First Ladies at the Smithsonian

americanhistory.si.edu/exhibitions/small_exhibition.cfm?key=12 67&exkey=863&pagekey=864

Take a virtual tour of the exhibit on the First Ladies at the National Museum of American History.

First Ladies' Trivia

www.firstladies.org/DidYouKnow.aspx

Learn fun facts about America's First Ladies at the website for the National First Ladies' Library.

Publisher's note to educators and parents: Our editors have carefully reviewed these websites to ensure that they are suitable for students. Many websites change frequently, however, and we cannot guarantee that a site's future contents will continue to meet our high standards of quality and educational value. Be advised that students should be closely supervised whenever they access the Internet.

Index

JAN   2015

Clifton Park-Halfmoon Public Library, NY

0 00 06 04474171